D0591199

Disney
VILLAINS

THE ESSENTIAL GUIDE

GLENN DAKIN

DK

"I live for furs... I worship furs!"

CONTENTS

"Just you wait until I get you in my coils!"

"...I must continue my search for the helpless Man-cub!"

INTRODUCTION
by Captain Hook

AHOY THERE YOU BILGE RATS! Do you hate happy endings? Does it make you sick when the beautiful princess marries her handsome prince? Does it drive you mad to see the hero defeat the villain and make him look silly in the process? No? Well, it ought to! Here at last is a book that celebrates all the mean antics of the vilest villains you ever met! Swoon at our loathsome looks! Gasp at our diabolical deeds! And cackle at our rotten jokes! I just know you're going to love hating every one of us!

"All aboard, y'swabs, it's going to be one scary ride!"

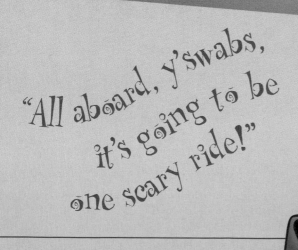

NAME: *Ursula*
OCCUPATION: *Sea witch*
(see pages 32–35)

NAME: *Scar*
OCCUPATION: *Lying lion*
(see pages 36–39)

NAME: *Evil Queen*
OCCUPATION: *Sorceress*
(see pages 6–9)

NAME: *Shere Khan*
OCCUPATION: *Stripy stinker*
(see pages 28–31)

NAME: *Sid*
OCCUPATION: *Toy torturer*
(see pages 42–45)

NAME: *Cruella De Vil*
OCCUPATION: *Dognapper*
(see pages 22–27)

NAME: *Maleficent*
OCCUPATION: *Scary fairy*
(see pages 18–21)

WICKED QUEEN

MAGIC MIRROR ON THE WALL, who's the meanest hag of all? Snow White's wicked stepmother, that's who! Not only is she an evil queen, but she's a wicked witch as well, with a laboratory full of potions that would make your blood freeze! Prepare to be scared out of your wits....

Now That's Heartless!

The Queen is so jealous of Snow White's beauty, she forces her to dress in rags and work as a scullery maid. When the Magic Mirror says that Snow White is still fairest of all, the foul fiend orders her faithful Huntsman to cut the poor girl's heart out!

MEANEST MOMENT – Feeding a poisoned apple to Snow White, and being cruel enough to tell her it would make all her dreams come true!

ACHILLES' HEEL – Her jealousy. She's so mad with envy she doesn't realise her evil plans will end in her own downfall.

PET PEEVE – Dwarfs. Much too jolly and too fond of Snow White!

It's a good thing the hunter spares Snow White and fools the Queen with a pig's heart instead! (Wonder how the poor pig felt about it?)

Black cloak helps the Queen blend in when she's lurking in the shadows

Snow White's popularity also drives the Queen crazy. Even when Snow White is lost in the forest, she finds herself a new fan club - of admiring Dwarfs.

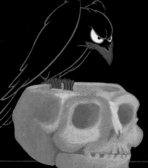

The raven is the Queen's pet and knows all her secrets. When things get too scary he hides inside a skull for a spell.

Blood-red lipstick is a vital part of an evil queen's beauty regime.

💀 Demon Drink

The Queen's evil plan requires her to drink the "Peddlar's Disguise" potion, which transforms her into a scary old crone. Of course, vain Queenie thinks she looks like a kindly old granny.

A potent potion transforms the Queen, but frankly this is pretty close to how she looks without her make-up anyway.

"Mummy dust, black of night, old hag's cackle..."

Box for putting hearts in

Purple is a colour of royalty.

Next, old knobbly-nose cooks up a poisoned apple. Whoever takes a bite will catch "the Sleeping Death," and be buried alive!

DUNGEONS OF DREAD

To her subjects, she is simply a proud, cold-hearted Queen. Little do they suspect that underneath her throne room is a labyrinth of dark passages, a place of echoes and shadows that many have entered, but few have escaped from! Creep in and take a look around....

Magic Mirror

Hanging in a secret chamber is the Queen's prized possession—a Magic Mirror. When she stands before it, a face appears in a puff of smoke and asks her, "What wouldst thou know, my Queen?"

"As proud as a peacock" the saying goes—this vain Queen even has one carved onto her throne.

The Magic Mirror is decorated with symbols of the zodiac.

Secret staircase known only to Queen (and rats).

The Queen's coat of arms is a creepy image of crowns and snakes.

The jealous Queen is so vain she only ever asks one question: "Magic Mirror on the wall, who is the fairest one of all?"

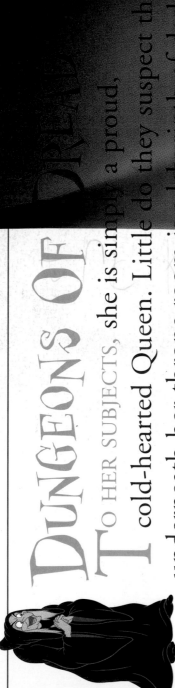

Lightning Exit

For a moment the Queen is victorious as Snow White bites the apple, but the forest creatures have already warned the Dwarfs of her evil antics and soon the pop-eyed crone is forced to flee for her life....

The Queen plans a spot of Dwarf-splatting with a boulder she has found—but the ledge is shattered by lightning and she plunges to her doom. Good riddance!

Meanwhile, Snow White is kissed by her handsome prince and looks well on the way to living happily ever after.

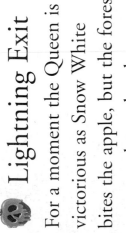

"It's a magic wishing apple," lies the shrivelled old sourpuss. But she doesn't realize that soon all Snow White's wishes really are going to come true!

Looks like the escape plan failed

The pet raven likes to have a good view of all the horrible goings-on.

Spell Books (mostly overdue from the Witches' Library)

Skeleton scales for measuring out nasty ingredients for potions

CAPTAIN HOOK

He kidnaps princesses, makes young girls walk the plank and even shoots his own men for singing. He's the scourge of Never Land, and only Peter Pan can keep him in order. Swoggle me eyes, it's Captain Hook, of course!

Pure piracy

Captain Hook is the wickedest pirate that ever sailed the seven seas. This one-handed buccaneer has one desire in life – to rid the world of Peter Pan! Why? Because Pan fed the captain's left hand to a crocodile years ago, forcing him to wear a blasted hook!

Duelling with Hook is just a game to Peter. With a pinch of pixie dust, Pan can fly circles round his enemy.

Peter Pan

The boy who never grew up, Peter is the real master of Never Land. Friend of the Indians, hero of the Lost Boys, and adored by Tinker Bell, he protects everyone from Hook's wicked plots.

Peter is a great impressionist and can give orders in a voice just like Cap'n Hook's!

Hook carries his cutlass with him everywhere.

Tick, tock, tick, tock… watch out Captain, the crocodile that ate your hand (and swallowed your alarm clock!) is still after you.

Hook's flamboyant hat sports an ostrich feather.

"Blast that Peter Pan!"

The vain captain fancies himself as a great charmer and even manages to con Tinker Bell into believing he is her pal.

This dandy pirate is always smartly turned out in his best dress coat with gold trim.

MEANEST MOMENT – Too many to choose one, but sending Peter a time bomb disguised as a present from Wendy is one of his lowest tricks!

ACHILLES' HEEL – He is terrified of the crocodile, and the slightest sound of its alarm clock ticking will turn the pirate into a gibbering wreck!

PET PEEVE – Being called "Codfish."

Smee never gets a big enough share of the treasure to afford fancy gear.

Soft-hearted Smee

Smee is Hook's right-hand man, always ready with a cheery word or a wicked plan to cheer up his "Cap'n". This sentimental scallywag is such a muddlehead, he sometimes lets prisoners escape by mistake!

THE JOLLY ROGER

LOOK ALIVE, YA SWABS! Here she is, the scourge of the seven seas, Captain Hook's pride and joy. Loaded with enough cannons to sink a navy, enough grub to feed an army, and enough grog to give the whole crew a nasty headache every morning – it's the Jolly Roger!

Pirate Paradise

Yo ho ho, it's a grand life aboard the Jolly Roger – if you're a scurvy sea-dog that is! You have the honour of sailing with the world's most famous pirate, and you get a free skull-and-crossbones tattoo on signing up!

Captain's Orders

1. No singing.
2. No blasted cheerfulness!
3. No mentioning of that brat Peter Pan.
4. No pet crocodiles!

Cap'n. Hook

Despite having the swift ship on the waves, Hook drives his crew batty by never sailing anywhere! All he wants to do is hunt for his arch enemy – Peter Pan.

Cannon set with a short fuse for quick-fire action

With no ships to sink, the bored buccaneers spend their days singing and dancing or practicing their ng – at pictures of their "beloved" captain.

THE CAP'N

Skull figurehead to strike terror in foes' hearts

Sinister skull
emblem

Lanterns are
sometimes useful
for imprisoning
fairies.

Pirate in
crow's nest on
the lookout
for Pan

Hook's luxurious
cabin with his
piano, his fine
treasures, and
a bucket in
which to soak
his feet

Crews' quarters
are generously
shared with fleas,
lice, and nits.

"Aye, aye, Cap'n!"

Secret store of spare
cutlasses, gunpowder,
cannonballs,
booty and rum

NEVER LAND

S ECOND STAR TO THE RIGHT,
and straight on till morning –
that's the way to find Never Land.
But take care, this enchanted place is full of
surprises and perils for the unwary. Take a
look at our map based on Captain Hook's
own secret charts....

Hangman's Tree is
the secret entrance to
Peter Pan's hide-out.

Hangman's Tree

Indian camp

Peter joins in a tribal
dance, with Tiger Lily
and the Lost Boys.

Blackfoot tribe

Never Land is home to a playful tribe of
Indians, belonging (according to Wendy's
brainy brother John) to the Algonquin
group. Horrid Hook sends their chief on
the war path by bagging poor Princess Tiger
Lily and holding her hostage.

This sunny isle may
look peaceful, but
it is constantly
overrun by pirates
hunting for pesky
Peter Pan!

Pretty waterfalls are
just one part of Never
Land. It is also home
to grouchy bears and
rampaging rhinos.

Skull Rock is Hook's favourite haunt for leaving captives tied-up and waiting for the tide to come in... what a meanie!

Mermaid Lagoon is a good place to spot Peter Pan, as he often drops in to chat with the mermaids.

Despite the happy smiles of the pirates, walking the plank is no joke with crocodile-infested seas!

*Skull Rock
(behind volcanoes)*

Waterfalls

*Mermaid
Lagoon*

*Blindman's
Bluff*

*Crocodile
Creek*

Peg Leg Point

The Jolly Roger often lies at anchor in the sheltered bay known as Cannibal Cove.

Hook's Downfall

In a final battle, Peter Pan and Captain Hook battle it out on the rigging of the Jolly Roger. Defeating his foe, Pan is prepared to be merciful, but the cowardly captain tries a sneaky attack from behind. He misses and tumbles into the sea.

"Smeeeeee!"

Hook is last seen swimming for his life, as he is chased over the horizon by the hungry crocodile. One consolation for the panic-stricken pirate is he does finally find his old alarm clock halfway down its mouth!

VILE VILLAINS

MAD MARAUDERS, evil explorers and even beastly butlers – the human race has produced evil-doers of every shape and size! Here's a selection of some of those sinister stinkers who just love to stand in the way of happy endings!

"Here Kitty!"

MISERABLE MEANIE

Lady Tremaine pampers her own diabolical daughters, while making poor Cinderella slave away at the chores all day. She also tries to stop her from going to the Prince's ball... luckily without success!

SLIMY SERVANT

Don't let his polite exterior fool you – Edgar the Butler is a ruthless cat-hating monster, who will quite cheerfully do away with a few "Aristocats" if it will help make him rich. Don't worry, as a fiend he's a big flop!

SLY SHOWMAN

Stromboli is an evil puppet master who keeps his star Pinocchio in a cage at night to stop him running away. As if that wasn't rotten enough, he threatens to chop Pinocchio up for firewood as well!

HOPELESS HUNK

The strong, stupid type, Kronk is Yzma's right-hand man and co-conspirator in her attempt to do away with Emperor Kuzco. Kronk's bungling means they only succeed in changing him into a llama!

MERCILESS MERCENARY

Commander of the force sent to discover Atlantis, Captain Rourke will stop at nothing to steal the power-source that protects the lost land.
Like Atlantis, his plans are well and truly sunk.

DASTARDLY DIGGER

He may just be a toy, but the Prospector is every bit as tough as a real gold prospector —s as Woody soon finds out.

HORRIBLE HAG

Yzma is poisonous from the tip of her ludicrous feathered hat to her wrinkly grey toes. She's set on destroying the spoiled Emperor Kuzco and behaving even more badly in his place.

"How many times do I have to kill you, boy?"

VICIOUS VIZIER

Not satisfied with being top advisor to the Sultan of Agrabah, greedy Jafar wants to marry the Princess, steal Aladdin's genie, and become the most powerful sultan in the world! Naturally, he ends up being the biggest loser.

MALEFICENT

YOU WOULDN'T LIKE

Y her when she's angry... this fiendish fairy turns into a scary fire-breathing dragon! Mistress of the Forbidden Mountain, Maleficent enjoys bossing her dim lackeys around, putting curses on newborn infants, and making life tough for the good fairies.

"You poor, simple fools, thinking you could defeat me... the mistress of all evil!"

With slaves to do her bidding, Maleficent has plenty of time to paint her nails.

Just like the wicked Queen in *Snow White*, Maleficent's favourite pet is a raven. It all goes to prove that wicked witches are all raven mad!

Aurora grows up to be a sweet, happy young woman, which is pretty sickening for moody old Maleficent!

Mighty Miffed

Maleficent is so angry at not being invited to Princess Aurora's birth celebration, she casts a spell on the poor baby. The curse states that on her sixteenth birthday, Aurora will prick her finger on a spinning wheel and die!

Never trust anyone who wears a two-horned hat!

Pale green skin: very fashionable among evil fairies

Big-headed Maleficent likes to have the showiest magic wand ever.

Lazy pet raven hitches a ride on Maleficent's shoulder

Maleficent finds it quaint that King Stefan invites the good fairies to his party.

"Touch the spindle!" commands Maleficent and the princess is soon plunged into a deep slumber.

Jagged wing-like robes are a clue to dragon powers

MEANEST MOMENT – Putting a curse on Princess Aurora. What a foul birthday present!

ACHILLES' HEEL – Trusting her brainless slaves. Sixteen years after being sent out to find Aurora, the bungling goons were still looking for a baby!

PET PEEVE – Being unpopular. She hates being left out of parties and is no good at pretending she's not offended.

Forbidden Mountain

TOWERING OVER Forbidden Mountain is a fortress bristling with needle-sharp towers, festooned with grotesque gargoyles, and populated by a gibbering horde of nitwits. Still, Maleficent seems to like it that way....

Maleficent masterminds the search for Aurora from the highest tower.

A mighty drawbridge is the only entrance to the evil fairy's domain.

Maleficent's blockheaded goons are created by her own magic out of pigs, bats, and any other creepy critters she finds crawling around near her garbage bins.

Hero Time!

Only Prince Phillip can awake the princess with true love's kiss. The vile villainess tries to stop him by throwing a ring of thorns around the king's castle. Here comes the showdown!

"Sword of Truth fly swift and sure!" Flora gives Prince Phillip the edge he needs to tackle the evil fairy in dragon form!

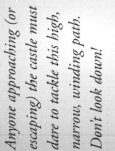

Anyone approaching (or escaping) the castle must dare to tackle this high, narrow, winding path. Don't look down!

Hot Stuff

The evil fairy's big party trick is turning into a dragon. In this shape, Maleficent thinks she is unbeatable. Well, it does improve her looks!

With Maleficent planning flame-grilled hero, romance might be off the menu for the happy couple!

That's got to hurt! Maleficent didn't think about the power of good magic over evil! Punctured by the Prince's sword, the old windbag falls into the fiery chasm. Hurray!

Why I Loathe the Good Fairies
by Maleficent 8. Fairy

1. Flora—this soppy do-gooder and the is crazy about flowers and she's kind to color pink—yuck! She's kind to babies, too!

2. Merryweather—so bright and jolly, she makes you sick! And she's always ruining my best curses. The spoilsport!

3. Fauna—like all good fairies she can only use her magic for good causes. Boring! It's much more fun turning into a dragon and scaring people senseless!

CRUELLA DE VIL

IS SHE A VAMPIRE? Is she a witch? No, she's just a spoilt aristocrat who's simply crazy about furs! The more beautiful the animal, the happier she is to see it skinned and turned into a trendy fashion item! And she will go to any lengths to get what she wants....

Dastardly Dognapper

Owning a Dalmatian fur coat is Cruella's dream and she is prepared to steal almost a hundred poor little puppies to satisfy her evil desires. Fortunately her plans are dogged by bad luck!

Don't be fooled when you see Cruella admiring this picture of Pongo and Perdita. She is only drooling over their "perfectly beautiful coats"....

Favourite coat made from rare arctic fox fur

MEANEST MOMENT – Ordering the death of the 99 puppies at Hell Hall. Her suggestions include poisoning, drowning and bashing them on the head.

ACHILLES' HEEL – Her impatience. Cruella hates waiting for anything. She does everything in a mad rush and it always ends up in disaster - for her.

PET PEEVE – Being surrounded by idiots! Snooty Miss De Vil is convinced everyone in the world (except her) is an imbecile.

Rats!

Cruella is only really happy when she is in a foul mood. She can even get crabby with a cute newborn puppy. When Perdita's litter is born without spots, Cruella calls one of the pups a horrid little white rat!

Cruella's unique hairdo shows her obsession with everything black and white.

Cigarette holder: old chimney breath thinks this makes her look stylish.

Fur handbag decorated with real tails – yuck!

Miss Moneybags thinks everything and everyone can be bought with a fat check. She blows her top when she finds out she's wrong!

Plain black dress to offset her beloved white furs

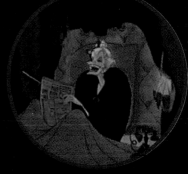

When Cruella isn't making life a misery for everyone else she likes nothing better than to sit in bed in her fur dressing gown and read about the trouble she's caused.

Pointy shoes match her spiky personality.

"Police warning! Keep your puppies indoors! Especially cute spotty ones!"

HELL HALL

HELL HALL, the sinister family home of the De Vil family, is just the place for dark deeds – like planning to bump off 99 cute puppies! Take a peek inside its gloomy walls....

Jasper is a weaselly waster.

Horace is a lazy lout.

Valuable portraits are now used by Cruella's henchmen for target practice.

Horace and Jasper are two pea-brained crooks hired by Cruella to steal the puppies.

Once the residence of great lords, the hall is now home to cobwebs, rising damp and rats.

Rotten Old Ruin

As Cruella would rather spend her cash on tasteless furry fashions than on the upkeep of the hall, her ancestral home is now falling apart at the seams. The fact that the place is such a ruin helps the kidnapped puppies make their escape, as there are so many dark places to hide in and helpful holes to wriggle through.

"I don't care how you kill the little beasts, but do it!" Cruella issues her orders to her blundering underlings.

This crumbling old mansion lurks on the edge of a forest in the county of Suffolk, just north of London, where Pongo and Perdita live.

Filthy windows last cleaned in 1872

Dust-covers draped over the antique furniture show that the once magnificent home is now unused and unloved.

Window frames riddled with woodworm

Huge hole in roof lets rain pour in

Damp walls are covered in moss

ESCAPE FROM CRUELLA

A BAT OUT OF HELL travels a lot slower than Cruella De Vil at the wheel of her Rolls Royce. All her hatred of obeying rules and seething rage at the obstacles in her way erupts to the surface as she leaves a trail of destruction in her wake....

The Hagmobile

Cruella's luxury car is ideally suited for gently cruising along the byways of England. Typically, demonic Miss De Vil has had it custom made to suit her own explosive character! Care to take a closer look?

Driven to destruction: Cruella careens out of control in her pursuit of the puppies.

Hook for her ghastly fox-tail handbag

Box of doggie-chocs to lure poor puppies into her cage

Poor Lucky shivers in the cold as the Dalmatians flee from Cruella. Don't worry, a safe, warm home soon welcomes them!

Monogrammed hub caps with Cruella's initials

Wing mirrors: Cruella never uses them.

🐾 Up in smoke

The chase for the pups finally ends when careless Cruella crashes into Jasper's truck. Her plans end in a pile of smoking debris in the snow.

"Aw, shut up!" After bumping into his evil employer, Jasper finally gets tired of being called an idiotic imbecile.

"We'll find the little mongrels, if it takes until Christmas!"

POLICE REPORT

№ 2378

Dangerous Driving
Miss Cruella De Vil
Suspect failed to slow down at the bridge and proceeded to crash through a barricade into the gully.

Miss De Vil reversed out of snowdrift and onto main road, destroying several fences in the process.

Finally, suspect collided with truck and crashed into a field, creating angry scene with the driver of said truck.

When apprehended, Miss De Vil said something unrepeatable about the police.

PC Dodds
PC234

The bare facts of Miss De Vil's reckless road-hoggery, as they appeared on the police record.

Miss Cruella De Vil
DAL 2356789

Clip-on ashtray and cigarette holder

Souped-up engine for high-speed getaways

Horn: mainly used for frightening people

Personal mascot and good-luck charm

Bumpers: constantly being repaired after crashes

SHERE KHAN

MAN-CUBS BEWARE! It's always bad luck when this cat crosses your path! Bears back off and monkeys flee for the treetops at the merest whisper of his presence. He's not all bad though. As well as being fearsome, Shere Khan is always fearfully polite – before he eats you.

Keen yellow eyes can spot prey in dense jungle

Brought up in the wild by a pack of wolves, Mowgli is not the easy prey Shere Khan is used to hunting....

Sharp lower fangs for gripping and shredding

"...Everyone runs from Shere Khan!"

Beard of white fur gives Shere Khan a distinguished appearance

Shere Khan is on the hunt for a Man-cub, lost in the jungle. The tiger thinks Mowgli will be easy prey, but he didn't count on the boy's many friends, including Baloo the fun-loving Bear.

Stripes help Shere Khan to blend in with the shadows of the jungle.

Trust In Me

Another jungle villain is the sneaky snake Kaa. This many-coiled creep uses his special hypnotic powers to lull his prey to sleep, then swallows them whole!

Paws conceal deadly claws that can be unleashed in an instant

The tiger likes to think of Kaa as his informer, but Kaa will happily lie to Shere Khan when there's a chance of a meal involved!

MEANEST MOMENT – Savaging Baloo to within an inch of his life. When the lovable bear defends Mowgli, Shere Khan shows his claws!

ACHILLES' HEEL – Fire! Despite his sophisticated veneer, Shere Khan is just a scared kitty-cat when faced with flames.

PET PEEVE – Being called "Old Stripes", usually by the cheeky vultures who sensibly stay out of Shere Khan's reach.

SHERE KHAN'S KINGDOM

THE TIGER IS KING of the jungle in the rainforests of India, and Shere Khan demands respect wherever he hunts. What he doesn't expect is a Man-cub without enough sense to be scared of him!

The Hunter and the Hunted

Mowgli manages to keep one step ahead of Shere Khan by hanging out with Bagheera the panther, Baloo the bear, King Louie, and even joining Colonel Hathi's Elephant Patrol – until he fails a routine trunk inspection!

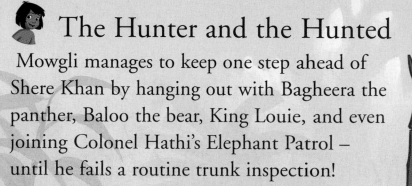

SHERE KHAN ON MAN-CUBS

Now I'm a reasonable chap and I'd like to give you my perfectly good reasons for eating Man-cubs...

1. A Man-cub will - if allowed - grow into something very unpleasant... a man!

2. A Man-cub will soon learn how to make fire. Fire spreads fear, terror and destruction throughout the jungle... which, let's face it, is supposed to be MY job.

3. Man-cubs taste NICE.

Mowgli is finally tracked down at the Black Pool, one of Shere Khan's top lunching spots.

Mowgli aims to safely reach the Man-village... if he doesn't end up in Shere Khan's stomach first!

Hey, friend, want to know how to make a tiger mad? Well, pulling his whiskers and calling him a pussycat are a vulture's top methods!

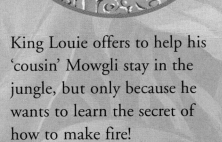

King Louie offers to help his 'cousin' Mowgli stay in the jungle, but only because he wants to learn the secret of how to make fire!

"Run, Mowgli, run!" Brave Baloo grabs a tiger by the tail and tries to give this pal time to escape. But Mowgli doesn't want to run away....

Can anyone smell roasting tiger? When lightning strikes a dead tree, Mowgli is given the weapon to drive his enemy away. 'Old Stripes' hot foots it from the scene with a burning branch on his tail!

URSULA

TWO-FACED AND terribly tricky, this devious denizen of the deep is a slimy, tentacled sea witch. Watch out if she offers to make your wishes come true... there's always a catch!

🐚 Banished Long Ago

This soggy sorceress was once a favourite at the court of Triton, king of the sea, until one day she was sent into exile. Ever since then, Ursula has sworn to overthrow Triton and rule the waves herself!

Triton has seven daughters, who are harder to rule than the rest of his kingdom! The real rebel is Ariel, a mermaid who yearns to be part of the surface world.

Flotsam, the eel, is Ursula's pet, and a slippery spy, too.

"Now I am the ruler of all the ocean!"

Figure-hugging black gown

URSULA'S BEAUTY TIPS

squid-ink eye-shadow

dead seaweed makes lovely false eyelashes

Soft Skin
A face pack of hand-pulped sea cucumber also makes a nice snack.

Hair Care
squished jellyfish makes groovy hair gel.

My Lipstick
squeeze a shellfish and the goo that comes out makes great lipstick.

Ursula is even cruel to other creatures when she's going through her daily make-up routine... as you can see from her beastly beauty tips!

Vile Vanessa

To prevent Ariel from marrying the man of her dreams, irksome Ursula tries to lure Prince Eric to the altar herself.
To do so, Ursula disguises herself as a mysterious beauty called Vanessa.

Ursula might change her face, but she can't hide her bad attitude – as a fight with Scuttle the seagull and his chums shows.

Magic yellow eye sends images back to Ursula's lair

The sea witch loves red-roe lipstick, fresh from the seabed.

Sleek hairdo for speedier slithering

MEANEST MOMENT – Saying she will help Ariel, but planning to steal her voice and her soul instead! Oh, and her dad's kingdom, too.

ACHILLES' HEEL – Her vanity. Ursula thinks she is so all-powerful, nothing can stop her. Prince Eric proves her wrong....

PET PEEVE – Not being invited to palace feasts. Old greedy-gills thinks she is so slim she is practically wasting away to nothing!

Jetsam is Flotsam's twin and constant companion.

Part octopus, Ursula actually only has six tentacles.

UNDERWATER LAIR

EXILED FROM THE SEA KINGDOM, and with her wicked mind seething with plans for revenge, Ursula was forced to find a secret place in which to hide away. In the darkest, creepiest trench in the ocean, she discovered a terrifying skeleton... and called it home!

Dragon Den

Ursula's lair is built within the rotting remains of an extinct dragonfish. She spirited away a few tons of rotting flesh (rumour is she actually ate them). Then, she had a nice cosy cadaver to settle down in.

Ursula's "little poopsies" (Flotsam and Jetsam) lure Ariel back to the sea witch's dark domain.

"What I want is your voice!"

When Triton barters his own soul to save Ariel, Ursula really does become Queen of the Sea.

Fanged entrance hall strikes terror into all visitors.

The garden of lost souls, where Ursula's victims are imprisoned

Giant shell lounger: Ursula's favourite place to lie back and put her tentacles up.

Dressing table and mirror

🐚 Shipwrecked

Growing to a massive size, Ursula prepares to destroy all her foes with the powers of Triton's trident. But Prince Eric sails a wrecked ship straight at her, piercing her bloated body with the tip of its broken mast. Ouch!

Those of you who hate happy endings, please turn away! With Ursula gone, Triton is once more king of the sea. All the poor souls are released from Ursula's lair, and Ariel (you guessed it) marries her handsome prince!

The crystal ball, beaming back images from Flotsam and Jetsam, floats in the witch's cauldron.

The stormy seas swallow Ursula's body, and soon the proud queen is just another dish of barbecued octopus for the bottom-feeders to dine on. And let's face it, there's a lot of her to go round.

SCAR

FEARLESS, NOBLE AND PROUD — these are three words that will never be used to describe sneaky Scar. This lying lion was first in line to be king until his nephew Simba was born. Now Scar will stop at nothing until he is top cat at Pride Rock.

Simba, the cub who would be king, is Scar's biggest enemy. Naturally the two-faced villain pretends to be Simba's best pal.

MEANEST MOMENT – Luring King Mufasa to his doom by putting Simba in the path of a stampede, then convincing the trusting young cub it was *his* fault!

ACHILLES' HEEL – Scar's weakness is that he just loves telling lies. In the end, nobody trusts him, not even his private army of hyenas.

PET PEEVE – Being told what to do by bossy old banana-beak, Zazu.

Personal fly swatter

Cackling Cronies

These heinous hyenas are Scar's henchmen, paid in tasty zebra steak. Luckily, the selfish slackers are too busy arguing among themselves to do much damage and bungle every attempt to do away with Simba.

Scar only uses his claws in an unfair fight.

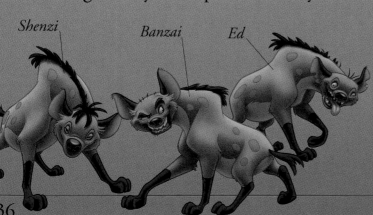

Shenzi

Banzai

Ed

Scar practices being king by bossing around these laughing lowlifes in the stinking pit they call home.

Mean, green, jealous eyes

Major domo Zazu on Scar: "He'd make a very handsome throw rug... whenever he gets dirty, you could take him out and beat him!"

"As far as brains go, I got the lion's share!"

Twisted smile: don't trust it!

Mangy black mane: Scar is too lazy to groom himself.

Scar's Downfall

When the adult Simba returns from his exile to challenge Scar, the pride turn on their cowardly king. Fearing for his life, Scar admits that he really killed Mufasa, and Simba is innocent.

Tumbling off a ledge while fighting Simba, Scar lands amidst his old allies, the hyenas. He has delivered their final snack... himself!

Unlike other lions, who walk tall and proud, Scar has perfected a sinister slouch.

With his evil uncle out of the way, Simba becomes the new Lion King, and the Circle of Life keeps rolling on....

THE PRIDE LANDS

EVERY LAND HAS ITS STORY, and the Pride Lands tell a tale of one mangy lion and his low-down, mean, back-stabbing rise to power. Happily, they also tell the tale of his fall and suitably horrible end.

The Tree of Life, with Rafiki, the wise baboon, meditating underneath

Simba escapes from the hyenas by running through these thorny bushes.

The Gorge Wall: Mufasa saves Simba, but is sent to his death by Scar.

The desert: Simba fled here after his father's death. Luckily, Timon the meerkat and Pumbaa the warthog were there to give a helping paw (and hoof).

The Dead Tree: when Mufasa perishes, Scar tells Simba to flee, claiming it is all the cub's fault!

That Shadowy Place

Mufasa tells Simba that everything the light touches is the lions' kingdom. But on the northern border of the Pride Lands, there is a dark domain where elephant bones moulder among the stench of geysers and snickering of hyenas. Naturally, this nasty neighbourhood is where Scar loves to hang out.

Pride Rock: home of Mufasa's family

Scar's Cave: Don't enter here unless you have a good escape-route worked out in advance.

African Plains: Scar tricks Simba and Nala into racing across them to the forbidden lands....

The steep-sided gorge is a dangerous spot to be caught in and is avoided by most lions.

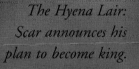

The Hyena Lair: Scar announces his plan to become king.

Entrance to the Elephant Graveyard: Simba and Nala don't know it, but this giant skull conceals three hungry hyenas.

CRAFTY CRITTERS

CRUEL CREEPY CRAWLIES

Cand conniving cats are among the villains in our bad-guy bestiary. Some of them may look cute, but one thing's for sure... none of these creatures are man's best friend!

"It's a bug-eat-bug world out there!"

CREEPY CONMEN

J. Worthington Foulfellow is a silver-tongued conman and Gideon is his lowlife assistant. This down-at-heel duo promise Pinocchio a glamorous life in showbusiness. But with the evil pair involved, there are always strings attached....

BULLY BUG

The insect world never produced a greedier gangster than Hopper. He believes ants only exist to collect food for the grasshoppers. Any resistance will be instantly squished – or so *he* thinks..!

MOLT

This klutz ruins the cool image of the grasshopper gang with his big mouth and clumsy antics. His brother Hopper would have smeared him long ago if he hadn't promised mum otherwise.

SLIMY SLEAZEBALLS

Nicknamed "Old Bad News", the Sheriff of Nottingham has great fun squeezing money out of the poor folk of Robin Hood's Olde England. Snivelling Sir Hiss is councillor to King John, and full of snaky schemes!

POWER-CRAZY CRY-BABY

While his brother King Richard is away, Prince John loves to rob the poor to feed the rich! He enjoys power and likes a cruel chuckle – until he runs into Robin Hood, who usually leaves John sucking his thumb and crying for his mummy.

"I'm having fish tonight!"

SENSITIVE SHARK

G'day, mates! Bruce is a great white shark who hopes to prove that all fish can be pals. He's a happy vegetarian, that is until he scents a whiff of blood – then he goes into a feeding frenzy! Fast-moving Marlin and Dory escape his jaws though, and go on to find Nemo.

TERRIBLE TWINS

Si and Am chase canaries, hunt goldfish and even try to steal milk from babies! It's a good thing that pampered pet, Lady, is doggedly determined to stop them!

CRUEL KITTY

Cinderella loves to watch the merry antics of the mice in her stepmother's house. So does lumbering Lucifer, who can't wait to pounce – and make their lives a misery!

SID

TOYS TREMBLE when they see this kid coming! Plastic soldiers retreat and dolls dash for cover. Sid's idea of playtime usually involves a brand new doll, a surgical mask, a pair of pliers, and maybe a firecracker or two. Be afraid....

"Let's go home and play!"

Short spiky haircut based on military action figure

Large forehead suggests big brain, all put to wrong use

Mirthless expression of experienced toy-tormentor

Buzz's helmet is down in case he rockets out of Earth's atmosphere.

Holiday Hell

When Sid is thrown out of summer camp early, it spells disaster for the toys awaiting him at home. Especially now that this twisted toy-torturer has figured out how to order explosive rockets through the mail....

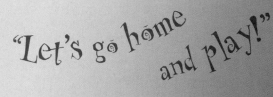

"Where are your rebel friends now?" Sid uses his magnifying glass as a weapon by turning pleasant sunbeams into searing heat rays!

Meet the happy, well-adjusted, fun-loving toys next door. Their worst fear is to end up as one of Sid's experiments.

Woody

Buzz Lightyear

Rex

Bo Peep

Mr. Potato Head

Andy, owner of Woody and Buzz, is kind and caring towards his toys, the exact opposite of Sid!

MEANEST MOMENT – Planning to blast Buzz Lightyear's atoms around the cosmos. Even evil Zurg hasn't gone that far!

ACHILLES' HEEL – His age. Despite being an evil genius, Sid is still just a kid and is quite likely to be called away from his wicked work by a call from his mum.

PET PEEVE – Being told on by his sister Hannah. Why do parents always take her side?

Blast Off?

When Buzz falls into Sid's clutches, the plastic space ranger is the obvious candidate to be shot into orbit on Sid's prize rocket, 'The Big One'. Woody, realizing he is about to lose a true friend, concocts a desperate plan to save him....

Deadly, toy-shredding jaws

"I have been chosen!"

Sid's dog Scud aims to be every bit as destructive as the deadly missile he is named after. As a special treat, Sid gives him toy aliens to chew.

SID'S LAB

Many toys enter but few leave

MANY TOYS ENTER but few leave unchanged... Welcome to Sid's room, where every dark cupboard conceals the hideous products of his twisted imagination. Take a tour, if you think you can face the full horror....

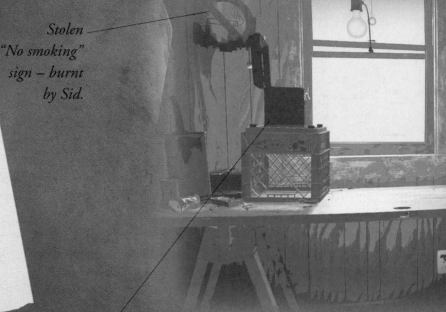

Stolen "No smoking" sign – burnt by Sid.

MOnDAY
Janie Doll in fOR double bypass
brAin transplant
(hEaD dOnoR :
Mr. Pterodactyl)

MaIN EVEnT:
Buzz Lightyear
set for BLAST OFF!

HOuston reports lAunch
ConDitions Looking Good

TNT

Tool box contains pliers, screwdriver, superglue and sticky tape, among other torture instruments

Here's Sid's workbench, or the Operating Theatre as he calls it. Once inserted into the vice, the patient is considered 'prepped' – in other words, prepared for surgery!

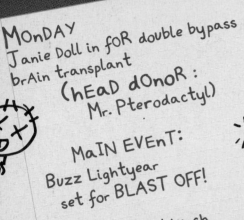

Woody's Round Up

Sid invites Woody to a barbecue – one he won't enjoy. To save himself (and Buzz), Woody has to call on the other toys for help, breaking all the rules and revealing the incredible truth: toys are alive! A terrified Sid runs for his life.

"Janie's all better now!" Sid creates a mutant toy out of sister Hannah's Janie doll and the head of a model pterodactyl. Sid takes his work seriously – he always wears a surgical mask and is assisted by an imaginary nurse.

Lava lamp: one of Sid's sickest inventions is this light made of illuminated severed heads.

Meet the Mutants

Sid combines broken toys into startling new creations. If there are no damaged toys around, Sid is happy to smash them up himself!

Ducky is the result of triple-toy surgery. Babyface is part doll, part erector kit. They may look scary, but are in fact kind and helpful when Woody needs them to be!

Stolen milk crates make great cages to imprison toys in.

Frog is used to distract Scud when the toys fight back

Long-buried toys arise zombie-style from the mud of Sid's yard to freak out their owner in a shock manoeuvre staged by Woody. Sicko Sid finally gets a taste of terror himself!

OUT OF THIS WORLD

FROM THE DEPTHS OF SPACE, the shadowy realms of myth, even from the toyshop on the corner – here come a whole horde of bizarre bad-guys. With their weird eyes, bad teeth and terrible dress-sense, they take us beyond the normal boundaries of scariness....

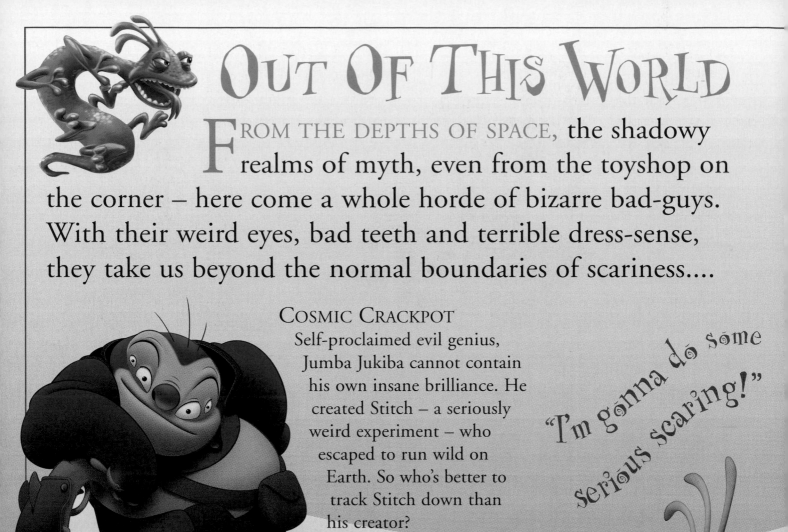

COSMIC CRACKPOT
Self-proclaimed evil genius, Jumba Jukiba cannot contain his own insane brilliance. He created Stitch – a seriously weird experiment – who escaped to run wild on Earth. So who's better to track Stitch down than his creator?

"I'm gonna do some serious scaring!"

MEAN MONSTER
Frightening kids was always a good honest job until Randall came along and cheated his way into the top spot at Monsters, Inc.! But it isn't long before Mike and Sulley discover his little secret....

BLOATED BOSS
Boss of Monsters, Inc., Henry J. Waternoose will do *anything* to make sure his energy plants keep producing scream-power for Monstropolis.

CUDDLY CYBORG

John Silver pretends to be the wickedest pirate in the Treasure Planet galaxy. But his soft heart is revealed by his fondness for his squidgy pet blob, Morph, and his new young friend, Jim Hawkins.

DEAD CREEPY

Hades, Ancient Greece's Lord of the Underworld, cannot resist a bargain, especially where there are souls involved. But his deal with Hercules is destined to end in disaster....

"Destroy Buzz Lightyear!"

SPACE SCUM

Meet Scroop, the most murderous member of John Silver's pirate gang. If there are dirty deeds to be done in space then this alien cut-throat is deliriously happy to do them!

EVIL EMPEROR

Enemy of the Galactic Alliance, Zurg enjoys toying with his sworn enemy, space ranger Buzz Lightyear. Zurg, who is poised to invade our galaxy at any minute, also claims to be Buzz's father.

47

DK

LONDON, NEW YORK, MELBOURNE,
MUNICH AND DELHI

Designer and Art Editor Anne Sharples

Senior Editor Simon Beecroft

Art Director Mark Richards

Publishing Manager Cynthia O'Neill Collins

Category Publisher Alex Kirkham

Production Controller Nicola Torode

Additional Art Marco Colletti

DTP Designer Dean Scholey

"This is an outrage!
Why aren't I
in this wretched book?!"

First published in Great Britain in 2004
by Dorling Kindersley Limited,
80 Strand, London WC2R 0RL

DK Australia
250 Camberwell Road, Camberwell, Victoria 3124

A Penguin Company

04 05 06 07 08 10 9 8 7 6 5 4 3 2 1

Copyright © Disney Enterprises, Inc.
Copyright © 2004 Disney Enterprises, Inc./Pixar
Animation Studios
Page Design Copyright © 2004 Dorling Kindersley Ltd

All rights reserved. No part of this publication may be
reproduced, stored in a retrieval system, or transmitted in
any form or by any means, electronic, mechanical,
photocopying, recording, or otherwise, without prior
written permission of the copyright owner.

ISBN 1-4053-0567-3

A CIP record for this book is available
from the British Library.

Color reproduction by Media Development and Printing, Ltd.
Printed and bound in Italy at L.E.G.O.

Acknowledgments
Mr. Potato Head® is a registered trademark of Hasbro, Inc.
Used with permission. © Hasbro Inc. All rights reserved.

Discover more at
www.dk.com

Gaston – the vain villain from
Beauty and the Beast.